COMMON GROUND

Books by Dabney Stuart

Poetry

The Diving Bell (1966)
A Particular Place (1969)
The Other Hand (1974)
Round and Round (1977)
Rockbridge Poems (1981)

for children

Friends of Yours, Friends of Mine (1974)

Criticism

Nabokov: The Dimensions of Parody (1978)

COMMON GROUND

Poems by Dabney Stuart

Louisiana State University Press
Baton Rouge and London 1982

Designer: Rod Parker
Typeface: Janson
Typesetter: Graphic Composition
Printer and binder: Thomson-Shore

Library of Congress Cataloging in Publication Data

Stuart, Dabney, 1937–
    Common ground.

    I. Title.
    PS3569.T8C6   811'.54   81–23659
    ISBN 0–8071–1023–x   AACR2
    ISBN 0–8071–1024–8 (pbk.)

Most of these poems, often in different forms, have appeared in the following publications: *Crazy Horse, Hampden-Sydney Poetry Review, Into the Round Air, Landscape and Distance: Contemporary Poets from Virginia, The Malahat Review, Michigan Quarterly Review, New Virginia Review, Paintbrush, Ploughshares, Prairie Schooner, San José Studies, Southern Poetry Review*, and *Southern Poetry: The 70's*.

"Mining in Killdeer Alley" appeared originally, in slightly different form, in the *New Yorker*.

"At the Circus, or Thereabouts," "Stacked up over Parkersburg," and "Will There Be Any Stars in My Crown" first appeared in the *Ohio Review*.

"An Interlude at the Grand Hotel," "The Life You Live May Be Your Own," and "Tell Me About Yourself" (now titled "A Note to Ben Jonson") were first published in the *Sewanee Review* 83, 2 (spring 1975). Copyright 1975 by the University of the South. Reprinted with the permission of the editor.

"Histories," "A Chance Encounter," and "Begging on North Main" first appeared in the *Southern Review*.

The italicized material and some of the factual allusions in "Dark So Early, Dark So Long" are taken from the Sunday, October 24, 1920, edition of *The North American*, a Philadelphia daily newspaper whose front sports page reported the Virginia Military Institute's "jolting" upset of the University of Pennsylvania, 27–7, the day before. My father played quarterback in the single wing, and defensive safety, for V.M.I., which was on its way to an undefeated, untied season.

Publication of this book has been supported by a grant from the National Endowment for the Arts in Washington, D.C., a federal agency.

for Sandra

and to the memory of my father

CONTENTS

Facing Up

Turnings

Common Ground

Facing Up

CUT OFF AT THE PASS

A curious man changes the measure of things:
Enters a space where there seemed room for nothing
Else, and creates reflections of surprise;
Transforms the tensile properties of gut
Into potential music, a violin,
And thus confounds the quick, the dead;
Seasons a novice, defies gravity, can rise
Into the pure weight of speculation
Where blithe nothing incorporates itself.

                                                    It's

Almost flight.

                    Are there lines which lead
                    toward the open chances
                        of such a life?
                    My own rare distances

                have become closed baggage
                trailing a shred, a loose ribbon,
                a tatter of my former self.
                                                A child
                        could follow it,
            must follow it, and, catching, unravel
                it to the innermost region
                        of his desire

                until I become a stranger

                        nothing

                    than I am

A new weave of air.
                        Fashion it that way, I said,
And a gang of derelict boys grabbed me.
I've had enough internal hemorrhaging, I said;
Take this, then, they answered, a heavenly choir,
And gave me a broom, made me balance it
On the end of my nose, point it at the sun,
And turn, turn, turn.

FACING UP

If you choose to return home by a route different
From the one by which you departed, no one
Will recognize you. It's likely no one
Will recognize you anyway, given the crowded air
And the way our memories blur and thicken.

I'd been on the same plane going away
What felt like years
When I finally found my place,
But the sign lying in it said *Occupied*.
Who could that be? I wondered, and saw
The sign on the restroom door flash the same thing.
I bent and looked out the window
At the collected poignance of the unique planet
Below me. This is no way to travel, I thought,
Whatever the direction, and
A rush of air, or light, took from me
What I gave and set me on the ground again.
I wasn't empty, I left that on the plane,
But I felt there must be more of me to come.

Yessir said a voice I'd never heard before
Seeming to drop from the sky as smoothly as I had.
Land's end. You can go hang
Upsidedown like a blind animal now, or sing
The Sunset Chorus and Universal Lamentation
As loud as you want to, but
There'll be no denying the echoes
Describing a head inside your head.
                                          I reached down
And cupped my sex in my hand, puzzled
But curious, thinking he didn't understand
Until he told me all echoes are severe
And a deaf man has no advantage
Simply because he hears nothing.
                                          Every creature
He said, *gathers at least once in his life*
To an urgency he has to serve; and I believe
Pain is not intended to be a human conveyance.

His voice thinned as he talked, seemed to go
Back into air. I'm not sure

4

Exactly who he was all that time, and I don't know
How to measure distance by a fading sound,

But I seemed to have come back where I had started:
No one recognized me anyway. Everything looked
As I remembered it, and I began
To wonder if it was my voice I had been
Listening to,
Until suddenly someone
Who seemed to be one, and legion, stood beside me,
And the voice out of the air before me said

      Well, then, I speak you wife and man;
        Go spin out life as best you can.

      And all the parties said

      Amen.

NO YELLOW JACKETS ON THE MOUNTAIN

for Mike Martin

Friendship turns. And turns again. Another name
For history, the mimes of history
                        end-
less
        exercises, webs of language
Preceding us, spun brotherhoods into which we fall
As we are born, learning to speak to each other.

Ten years ago you stopped chasing
The cities of the Western world as if they were women,
Abandoned the mazes of strasses and allées
And freight yards, and came back to Virginia
To build a cabin on Big Walker Mountain.
Since then I've climbed it a half dozen times
To speak with you, passing
The trail's forks and the forked trees, one tree
Writhing upward past its fractured limb, above
The bloodroot and wintergreen, until
I can dream it so clearly the whole ascent
Seems part of the talk itself, composed
—except for the light beyond the unsettled leaves
Casting these flickered shadows—as a poem
Is composed.
              And yet
The light in a poem
Is like no other light, nor like itself,
Shining as it does through a network
Which is also its source.
                   Can poetry
Glow in the dark, then? With darkness?
Can a friend? What kind of luminous mesh
Is strong enough to sustain the complexities
Of friendship? What is sufficient?
                      Your life
Seems to crumble
Like rotted wood to the touch.
One day the wind will rise
And disperse it over the mountain:
Have you wished for this from the beginning?
                       I remember
Your hand burrowing in a chestnut stump,

Fingering the cool loam, then suddenly withdrawn,
Already swelling with the hidden sting.
                                    And today

I climb the mountain again, leaning
Against its pitch, listing
Past broken
Causes, twisted
Growth, wanting again
To give it up, turn back, missing
The highwire joy that keeps a man
Working at these heights from letting go.

I rest on a rock. I find myself

Staring down at the valley, my eyes
Filled with the railroad tracks' dazzling
Twin silver, playing their usual trick
Of joining beyond sight, denying themselves.

Meanwhile, the blue shadows on the leaving trees,
The early petals, fallen, the predictable transactions,
Departures, a mountain cabin
—paper littering a table, a heated stone—
These are never sufficient, but they remain
Clues to places, or a place:
They too reflect a light.

DOING TIME

for John Adams

1

If my concentration is perfect
And I attain the exact tension
I can blind a man with one jab
From the tines of my index and middle fingers.

I need no other weapon to separate him from his life.

I can walk away.

On the other hand, the one in the mirror
And I can't do without each other.
I return to him like a bird to its nest
After turning the earth for worms,
Or he returns to me the same way,
It's hard to tell. When the mirror breaks
There will be a sound as of clods
Tinkling, and a fine rigmarole of dust
Will rise into the air, becoming air.

2

John, you know in ways I don't
How trouble can turn a man, drive him into the ground.

I hear you tell me again how the sky lowered
Toward you each morning at "the farm,"
As if to force you to your knees, seeming to say
You have flown, now pay for it.

You learned to handle the big Cats, heavier than earth
Moving the earth, driving birds from the scrub and hedges
You turned under, changing the face of things,
Your face.

The difficulty you had getting parole
Is no less a mirror in which we can measure ourselves
Than is the length of the sentence we gave you
For lifting 20 grand at gunpoint

And turning yourself in.
                              But you got it,
Turned around,
Walked through the gates, flashing
A smile out of your heavy beard, waving
As if to take off. Was the fork
You made with your first two fingers lifted
A sign of victory, or peace?

3

An illiterate, back-country musician
Who had begun to lose his touch on his autoharp
Asked the preacher to hold a service for him.
"Pray for my hands,"
He said, which was done, the whole county
Concocting a sound to make that immense journey,
Traveling the mysterious arc of the gathered voice
Outward where need whispers to itself, then bending
Back, translated, and within six months the musician's
Fingers were releasing bright notes
Again, one after another taking wing
Into his air from the strings he barred
And plucked, his uncaged fingers themselves
Fluttering. This is what is meant

By *the flight of song*, a feathering
Of our grave encumberments, and most of all,

During his moments of absolute attention,
Which are called music, he bends
Over his instrument as tomorrow bends over us,
Reflecting.
                He begins
To hear himself, again.

YOU CAN COUNT ON ME

As for the incident involving

The glass staircase, a man with a razor on the landing,
His imminence, my punching him
In the nose, his bloodless smirk,

I was no hero, but I appreciated the onlookers'
Taking time to thank me.
                                    Here at home
Everything's normal: as if nothing
Happened, the dog-day woman,
Intent on proving again she's a midwife for stones,
Comes skipping in the only way she can,
Along one of her tangents, singing
Careless Love, asking the familiar spot on the wall
Behind my shoulder what kind of a day it had.

Sometimes before she goes to sleep
She tells me stories which, whatever
Their plots, all end the same way
With the heroine saying to her male menagerie
Darlings, you are inept because you talk
To hear yourselves talk.
                                    She sleeps soundly
As a rule,
As if her regardless theory were a pillow,

But tonight I give her a dream
To account for: a man hovers palpably
On the transparent stair, the light glints sharply
From the blade he raises, her eyes burn with it
And she wakes, still in the dream, to find herself
Kissing the cracked knuckles of an anonymous hand.

A FIGURE ON THE ICE

for Joseph Garrison, Jr.

1

The last thing
I remember when I was a boy
In the North winter I'd line the barrels up
Sixteen or eighteen abreast across the pond
And back off, way off, and hone my blades and paw
At the ice, then skate full on, take soaring to the air,
And land on barrel four or five.
Dependably. I'd sprawl there
In the splinters and raw cloth and bent hoops,
And look up and say to you, *I made it*.
                                        That is,
I always wanted to, but never
Knew where you were.

2

As the skater picks himself up out of his debris
And replaces the barrels for yet another try,
Does he wonder, moving back to the beginning,
Whether he is making
Nothing
But a succession of interludes?
                                        If he does,
No gesture reveals it; he appears to go on
Measuring his prospects
By the same desire, looking up from the same success
Into the same absence.
                                        I'm not
As close to him as I used to be, but
I can imagine him still
Saying to himself,
                        *I'd like to
But I don't know where you are.*

3

As he takes off again
I slip away, leaving him suspended

In midair. The world before me
Differs:
            the slow hill I climb, the open field
Flecked with buttercups, a branching road.
If I find
Among the refracted curvings of the future
Someone to listen to this story
Will it matter, will I tell it
The same way
                —the skater turned
        inward to his figure, unaware he calls out
        come, applaud, release—
                        or will I tell
The truth, reveal my fear
Of that tenacious worm leaping in my colon,
Admit
        for the life of me
I can't put things together and need help?

A meadowlark whirrs upward from the field.

Behind me
I hear the ice begin to heave and split.

AT THE CIRCUS, OR THEREABOUTS

The trick to survival was to accomplish something of no utility,
and so small as to be inconspicuous.

The people who come here
Have designs, they follow each other
Under the big tent, becoming as much a part
Of the opening parade as any creature, the
Elephants, the painted ladies, web-footed clowns,
The torsos of air, the shortest man.
                                        Or the high-
wire walkers, whose attendance is perfect.
One of them goes up a ladder in the dark
To his perch, unremarked, while the other
Bobbles and totters up his access, the tilted guy,
Ten spots upon him. The band blurts and horns
His success. Then the two of them make a sort of love
Up there, trusting each other, equally lit,
Having only one common ground, and one way
To go, back and forth on that wire.

                                        Nobody
Amounts to much, son, teeth rot, and all the eyes keep
Right on remembering,
                        that's the way it is,

An incredibly silken body at this distance
Has the bit in her teeth, is arched from a rope,
And spins. I can't believe such lovely
Unbelief! Not a thought near her head, she's
Lutelike, a string in air,
                        the way it is,
That clown goes right on advertising his lies,
Comes right up to that green woman next to me
With his bubbling nose and that soggy luggage
Under his eyes and when she graciously puckers
Beyond all prediction,
                        he refuses the kiss.
                                        The living
End.
        Well,

The elephants have finished farting,
The lion tamer has crawled under his savage blanket,

Revlon is up a point, this heart his wonder
Has performed again, this jumpy heart,
This tough, unchewable, classic, Western muscle.

Would see, reader? Stay.

GAME, SET, MATCH

Given to reasoning, hard service, I suggested
To her that all games pit us
Against some part of ourselves, raised up
Like a net, like that net she leaves when the sun sets,
Or this one, between us, which never slackens.
                                        But it was like
Opening a closet and having the crammed words
Spill over me, like wading
Knee-deep through my own voice calling for help.

When I finally heard myself I decided
To make one last promise serve and said
The Shadow knows.
                        She stacked
All the balls she'd collected
On her side of the net, erecting a monument
Which she climbed, commemorating herself.
                                        When I left
Her sitting on top of it, looking into her racket
As into a mirror,

The keeper of the gate bowed to me, the sun
Seemed to disperse fine showers of gold
Through the clouds, and people called to me
Welcome Back,
Their voices rising in the open air.

A NOTE TO BEN JONSON

Ben, you've gotten thin. Your trunk is little more
Than a limb. Yet rare, you're as rare as ever.

The beasts of the field have slimmed thus, we have no mirrors
For their astonishment, they have not always been departing.

At Chorcorua 100 years ago nobody watched his weight.
It was decades before Sears' Exterior Latex
But the plump houses weathered obliviously.
The guests ate well. They talked. Deer grazed at the edge
Of the generous enclaves. In that large land, that *state*,
Even the flag was thick with the future, the trees
A green litany, the smallest hunger a sure step toward girth.
I have been swollen with
The bait from nostalgia's traps myself, these many years.

Will we see again how men can manage
With a little, Ben? How little?

Will we choose your needling diet, giving no quarter
To nature, pruning everything, as in your epitaphs? I

> Regard but do not understand
> The shuttered eye, the wasted hand.
> How does this little flesh disband?
> The time I buy, the names I sell
> Are nothing to this voided shell.
> What else is there to say? Farewell.

Bone voyage. So. Nature protrudes, regardless. Excrescences
To be reckoned with, I reckon, to be taken lightly

Or not, according to temperament, to be turned
To their most inward shape
In a second or third heat. And myself with them.

THAT'LL BE THE DAY

for Quentin Vest

1

Sweet Anna Gram is not
The lightsome plaything you like to think
She is. I go beyond
Zed and zygote, and there she is prancing,
Showing off, moving from one volute to another,
Denying nobody the smallest liberty, the smallest
Adjustment of illusion.
                For years
I thought she played to a packed house,
But I mistook the brilliance of the spotlights
Focused on her for the audience: I forgot
Use is not performance, and she is nothing
If not used.
           Nonetheless,
In all the parodies of vengeance the rest of us
Enact, no one approaches
The exquisite balance of her attention:

We say *live*, and she gives us *lie*
And *evil*, or
Is evil itself false? or
The whole composite
Vile? In *death* she hides our appetite,
In *love* a stringy rodent
Who can take all the tricks in the game.
                      These are
The big words, I'm trying to be honest,
                    live
Eat, love, die, are the permanent injunctions;

It's hard to imagine
She dances with them at random.

2

As long as it's someone else
Who's loving her, or saying so,
I can manage, but when I try to speak
To her, I have to cordon off the voices:

They don't quite echo each other.
They don't seek her the same way,
Or seek the same her, or seek anything
Beyond their own seeking sound.
                                        They aren't
Conscious of me. They stay on their side
Of the ropes, but I feel them threatening.
Haven't I sent you after her? Haven't I
Released you forever? I ask, multiplying
Them, dividing myself among them.
                                        Is this
Like life, I wonder, the lie
Cloistered in *belief*, the rut in *truth*, the truth
In everything, and like this, the cause
In *clause*, the am in *game* and *grammar*,
The increasing scar,
                        the tenure of return, the father
Disguising hate, what can I do with the rat
In generation?
                        No tentative man
In his right mind could create such a mob
And expect to survive it in one piece.

3

                        Anna,
This is goodbye. I'm calling
It quits. I'm going to be
Someone else. I don't care
If it is the same alphabet, I can learn
To make all my voices
Forget you. It doesn't matter
How the lines string out, how many syllables fondle
Each other in the dark
Wishing I were back, how often you don't exist
Because I don't talk you into it. It's not
My problem anymore. I plan
To become lovable, and move
Into the real world where nobody listens.

Turnings

BEGGING ON NORTH MAIN

Should I worry about choosing
The right word if I can get what I want
By pointing at it?
            What do I want?
                        Is it this ghost
With the unslakeable past, this rusty child
Who keeps asking me to give him his eyes back?

Is it the stone man who disappears
Beneath my toes every step I take,
Telling me he's nobody's thoroughfare?
                       If I were dreaming
Would I call them both *Father*
And follow them blind into the center of the earth?
Would I come out bright-eyed and raw on the other side
In a country whose people speak in pictures,
Where someone could say *Look*, and point,
And I would see my self?

It's hard to ask the right questions,
                       yet the fire I have
Kindled with my vocabulary and its hungry years
Gives off a growing heat,
                 and the day I saw
My reflection in its bottom I gave my tin cup
To the mute on North Main Street.
When he sees me coming he smiles
And points the cup at me, slowly turning it
Until it flashes the sun into my face.

BABY AND CHILD CARE

Listen, those of you with bones,
To the ceremonies of attention.

My first son, age six, hit his brother, age three,
With a baseball bat. When he had gone to bed
I asked him, severely, to remember
When *he* got hit with a baseball bat
Two years ago. He started to cry
And when I asked him what he was crying about,
He said *It hurts again.*
                 Able to leap tall buildings
                     at a single bound.

I have a lot of monkeys age three said.
You have a lot of words, too, I said.
He disappeared around the corner and I heard him walk
Through all the rooms of the house. When he got back
He asked *Where are they?*
                 More powerful than a loco motive.

But Superman's best gesture of rescue
Or prevention never matches the quickness
With which they close their gaps
Growing, extending themselves.
                       If
They aren't the masters of
My singing distance, they give me measures,

They keep a human time.

MINING IN KILLDEER ALLEY

for Nathan

One, and then another, they settled before me
　　like flakes of air,
Halfway up the hill, their splayed toes sketching
Shadows, the grass tufts, gravel, merging;
They came down from their marvelous fluency
To wobble on dumb stilts
Like earthbound creatures, hindered by strangeness.
The shadows were blue and voluminous, and their toes lost,
And the pronouns confused, and they shied and took flight
Again as I drove the rest of the way up the hill.
When I entered the house
And called my wife to the window they were back,
　　　　　　　　　　　　　　　　　　settled,
Settled into the dark; and in the Blue Ridge morning
They parted, again, for my descent.
　　　　　　　　　　　They were there
Every day the last seven months before the gift,
Feathering my passage
Like wings, their angled wings, her shoulder blades
As she bent awkwardly before the sink, mornings,
In the ninth month.

So that my father, who we thought was dying,
Could see him, we carried his newborn grandson
Up the back stairs of the hospital. The light was broken
All over the blanket, and our child swam in his glasses
With pieces of that broken light.
　　　　　　　　　　　Their russet throats,
The sun shattered in the gravel,
　　　　　　　　　　　the gray veins
Of his impeccable wrist,
　　　　　　　Lord, for the life of me.

When we brought him home they had flown away.

SNORKELING IN THE CARIBBEAN

Even as I seem to see
A school of angelfish it veers, dissolves, becomes
Mere coral, or sky-blue creatures of another eye
Than mine. My stillness centers
Nothing; it is impossible to follow
Such diversity of motion anywhere. I don't need
To go deeper than a foot to be lost, to be turned
Back into a creature of questions, prying
Shoreward, wondering

Would I live on snails and mussels?
Would I choose to starve? If I were about to be eaten
Would I defend myself so well
No one would recognize me anymore?
Would I try to become invisible? Is that the only way
To anticipate attack from any angle?
                              When
My son's foot was pierced by the spines of a sea urchin
The beach people told me I had my choice
Of going down on my knees before him and pissing on his wounds
Or binding him up and seeking out the amputator.
It wasn't prayer, but it worked.
For a week men glistening from the sea, muscled, lyrical,
Would stop and stare at his instep,
As if its pattern of black mottle were a fading sign,
A talisman, beyond questions, beyond belief.
                              Who
Could ask for anything more?
                    These creatures don't.
They continue to swim,
To eat.
They move away from me, they move
Away.
          If peace exists anywhere it exists here, under
Water
          —my ears fill with it, it leaks into my mask—
                                        where
What little that is asked is answered,
Always, under
Water,
          which I would raise
Like a goblet—this small bay containing everything

More or less—to you, brave child who refused to cry,
Whose pain my urine eased, who learns to swim
Behind a mask like mine.

TURNTABLES

for Darren

A grooved disc, a sliver of diamond, and the music rises;

His darkened eyes, the ribbon of birth
Cut: and the influential squawl
Thrilling the air
                —within which breath is drawn,
Within which the race is to the quickest,
Within which the race stories itself—
                         rises;

Above me today the dry air reflecting
The dry grass, a shimmer of heat between,
Inescapable. *Stand in this* the season says.
Neither air nor time grows into anything else
Though they circle forever, our lives lifting music.
Stand it says *where you are*:
                        in a small room
His small body, new in the air,
                  filling it;

The human music. The awful human music.

TWO ELEGIES FOR WALKER DABNEY STUART, JR.
(1901–1971)

I
Dark So Early, Dark So Long

> *The dead injure me with attentions,*
> *and nothing can happen.*

It's always too early,
No one is ever *quite* ready, but neither
Is a man to be measured by his intentions, the lordly avenues
He dreams of, the chimes, the fileted hour.
When the time comes, it comes.
                              The front
Of the mirror reflects my face, an expectation;
But if I turn the mirror over in my hand, its back
Reveals the back of my head. That's where I am,
In a center between expectation and surprise,
Where nothing happens.
                              My dead, your waking
Rocks me, waking.
                      What life was it
He was so devoted to? Every day his attendance was perfect,
But the files spill, the papers scatter;
Do his eyes stay closed in the locked dirt,
The meticulous box?
                      Do not
Mistake me. I have come
Here because I want

To come here. What I have
Lost compels me to

Come here. Someone
Has spirited away, all

Right, much. More.
It burns. Heat rises. Jack,

Be nimble, Jack,
Be quick, Jack,

Don't you know once dead there's no more dying?
Pull yourself together, here's Walker now, it's 1920,
                              he comes to play.
Though the Red and Blue schedules him as a breather
He comes to *shock 18,000 fans by ripping*
The Red and Blue to pieces, playing the best game
At quarter seen on Franklin Field this Fall;
                              he's suited up,
He moves through the broken field like a butterfly,
Does a Jubal Early down the sideline
With a stolen pass, soaring—
                    such heights,
Such luminous edges—
                    no Penn team
Was ever outclassed more or beaten worse
Than the Red and Blue eleven yesterday.
                              Yesterday.
The very word,
              death's feather in my cap.
                              And when the game
Ended, the seasons
Ended, the last reunion hale and golden ended, he comes home,
                    to my home,
Crosses my threshold, gives up what poise
Had let him dance that string of pearls,
Not once, but Lord these fifty years,

And I undress and dress and lay him down.

No more. My sorrow is not dead.

                              Do not mistake me.
I have come here because there is no other place.
It may be that death is peace, that the tiger
Lies down with the lamb, that the jackal
Speaks dulcetly with the mourning dove, that all
Will be well, and all manner of thing will be well,

But my tongue is dry, the nice quietude
Hemmed with thorns, and everything
Unseasonable, warped, unstrung.
                              When it's done
It is not done. I want to be quick, spirited myself,

To call toward the dread air irrational embodiments
Like
Hey Fulsome! Hey Guts!
You see this brand-new, second-hand flyswatter?
It's for you, and I'm a dead-eye with it; stay back,
This ain't no graveyard, you can circle like wide birds,
You can prey, yes indeedy, prey, but not on carrion,
No, on a source,
A light, a cluster of vitality, radiant, wheeling you,
And I'm right here in the middle singing shoo-fly,
Go away from my doors, my thresholds, the places where we
                                                         cross,
The bodies of my death my life.

It is not done until I say it's done.

II
The Life You Live May Be Your Own

Who knowes not Arlo-hill?

1

He has been undivided for a month:
He does not breathe.
His body does not tremble with the desire to breathe.
He is not seized, nothing seizes him;
He no longer angers himself by his dependence
On those who mistake their refusal to pity him
For love. I think he knew the difference,
But he didn't say.

An unobtrusive man who is responsible
For the success of others may compensate
For the praise he does not get publicly
By praising himself in private. Sometimes
He grows louder, more often. The focus of his stories
Closes toward a center. He seems repetitive, mere
Hot air. This is a form of desperation, a longing
For those measureless instants
When there was no audience,
An ineffectual rebuttal of time, as all our speaking is,
And no less worthy because it is common.

29

Remembering is not so much a desire to live something
Over again, as it is regret for having lived
At all.

The face of all earthly things is changed.

2

Old friend,

Swollen air, how we gone get *to* this gone
Old friend? His troubles are over no doubt
About that, he wheezed to the end
Of them, not least, nor the tossed rises, bone
Of his last dog's bed. I reckon he got out
And in about ten times a night, then he got out
Past time. Lord.
We got to deflate pard-
ner, learn how to say it straight one of these days,
Can't let it rest, bad doings, our first onliest stay
Against the world's most regiment done
Joined up. He wanted, finally, that. Say when.

3

It begins. It had begun
Before these words joined in their long distress,
Settling toward rhythm and its darker eye
As a stone through sinking water.

Even from down here I believe one day
My life will be full of a lot more
Than your death and its mordant dross,

Yet death is the talker's goad, or we'd be still
And our wayward voices creating everything
Would thin forever on the unsteady air,
No different from breath, which even dumb creatures draw.

TURNINGS

In the years of his growing loss he would walk
Through the rooms of the house after midnight,
The ice tinkling in a glass of bourbon
Accompanying him. Each door he passed
Through seemed to yawn him in, the quiet bodies
Of his sons unrecognizable in their dark beds.
He would sit beside them, making between his thumb
And fingers the smooth sheet give a soft, grating sound.

When he looked down at his wife's body in another room
The night itself seemed to yawn,
                                        so he went out into it,
Stood at the edge of the wide yard he'd tended for ten years,
Discovered the next largest darkness of all.
You are eating me alive, woman, he said softly,
Hearing himself.

In his teens
                —in some locker room
While he shrugged the sour pads on; or at the beach,
Watching some blonde mount her rowboat, between her legs
The humdrum wedge commanding her dumb male
Roll over, beg, yawning—
                                        he'd heard it said
If she's got long fingers and a big mouth
She'll be a tunnel of love.
                                He'd found it
So huge a tunnel it felt like falling, he'd found it
No place at all, and when he'd turned every way
He could think of, or imagine, and still touched nothing
He wanted to turn loose.
                                If he did, it seemed likely
His future would be committed to nostalgia for a time,
So, standing there watching the night expand,
Beginning to let go of it, he invented a past:

    Mythic, yet personal,
    Lined with down, but large enough for him
    To appear tough in. He experienced
    His first ecstasy doing the dishes,
    Her frothy hands laced on his nape,
    Her eyes dancing with light

Like the suds from liquid Lux: a maximum
Of foreplay, the aura of pineapple,
An infinite rising, the shadow of goodbye, aah . . .

To each his own, he thought, imagining
A mirror speaking
To the mirror across a room
About the arrangement inside the first mirror,
And so forth.

He pitched the diluted bourbon on the grass.

Neither the real fall nor the invention
Sounded like life, or a life he wanted,
Open for sweet returnings, and it did no good
To say quietly toward the window she slept behind
You are too much mouth. Go hang
Yourself on the doorknob by your teeth.
He had, after all, fallen of his own accord:
He remembered holding the small bodies of his sons
Newborn; he squeezed the empty glass,
Rubbing his thigh with it.
                              And having fallen
Could stand up again, and walk
Out of the tunnel's mouth as out of nowhere, somehow
Resume himself at least in the open air
Where he could see, and be seen, and not be consumed.

Absently he began to walk across the yard.
He touched the trunk of the white maple,
Brushed between his thumb and fingers a mimosa leaf,
Picked a crabapple. When he settled down
On the grass he let the glass roll away noiselessly
Not noticing the first fleck of sunrise glinting in it.

WILL THERE BE ANY STARS IN MY CROWN

When I chip the crystal river, bowed to it,
Its flakes sparkle their tight arcs skyward,
Even at midnight
—one son asleep above me—
Peaking, falling, they skid and twang;
If I stop it remains the same, one body clustered,
Symmetrical and frozen as the blessed
—the other across the room, reading.
                                        How
Do you imagine me, children? Can you see me seeing
Myself crouched here, my knife punctual,
My sleeves full of purpose, my hands releasing
This sweet light?
                    How patient must a man be, tending
His field, before he sees the sun feathered
In the meadowlark's breast, or
The collar of his sharp darkness?

He flies away from me.

The sun goeth down.

Ich warte.
                I can imagine one of them, reading the other
To sleep, and the other dreaming the first, reading.
Thus one voice moves in two worlds,
                                        brothers,
And even as my knees impress this ground
I sit between them, keeping the space open.
                                        Are we alike
In wanting the wind to rise, lifting these chips
Beyond the grave pressures molding us? They both sleep now
As I sleep in them, in this,

Rendering heaven.

LIFE WITH FATHER: A MEDLEY

Of old favorites? Well, not exactly.
Playing favorites isn't my favorite game,
Though I play, as people about me play
Theirs, keeping
Ourselves between each other and the light,
Holding the mirror sideways—
                                    human
Airs, all, defenses of a kind, perhaps this kind:

    My younger son is at his familiar songs
    Behind his bedroom door, in the dark.
    Nothing reaches me out here but the melody,
    Or the suggestion of melody,
    Lengthening the hallway.
    If there are words, I don't hear them.

    It is a kind of fending sleep,
    Wrapping in and wrapping out
    At once, he keeps
    Going back there, in the dark.

    When I'm in bed later tonight
    My voice here will sound
    Through a distance like the distance
    His travels now, the words gone,
    The melody coming from this dark
    To that, familiar.

Speaking of bedtime stories, and the longer dark,
There's the cartoon showing that old Boogieman
The Self, distended with longing, who searches
The penumbral bubble of his speech for that old Boogieman
The Self. Have you seen it? So have I. So will
My older son, sooner than I can imagine, to whom
I would say, knowing
How the beaten paths triumph and
The worn odds grow against him:

    It's not so bad
    To walk with your head down

    Because if one day you look up
    From the footsteps you think

You've been avoiding on the way
Through this dim jungle
And see yourself
Where you've always been,
Ahead of me,
Trailing,

You'll need the memories
To find the way again.
                              For myself,
A little child *shall* lead me, that's part of the password
Whatever twilights I move between; the trouble is
I confuse my sons with my childhood. And here
Is another open secret, a man may be misled
By his own expectations if he lets himself
Believe the long haul opens into anything
Except itself: true love

Is a mutual lightening of the lovers' solitudes,
Enmeshing darkness, deepened likenesses.
As for endangered species, the mirror could be misleading,
As could the daily round, its certain deductions:

                    My sons

        between the iced pane   and the cracked door

                    balance
                    their sleep.

    Woman, their ribs'
    Change,
    When you complicate this poise
    With your smooth divide,
    Its deep fire   the crinkling
    Years,
    At least
    Ransom them
    With sons   their sleep.

Perchance to dream,
                        a drifting off, a waning:
Through dreams a man learns nothing
Is irrelevant, the shapes of his sundering

Shift, merge, terms change, he begins
To pick up the pieces:

  —A place in the stream still
  Between pool and riffle where the moving water
  Seems to deny itself,
  A moment in which your cupped
  Hands dipping describe a dance
  Whose music is the motion of the stream—

  A space and time, children,

  To hold you in yourselves
  As a small smooth stone,
  Whose weight is the weight of the hand
  That holds it, is held in the hand,

  I offer in singing balance for that age
  When the world staggers your fine coherences.

Common Ground

HISTORIES

That I may reduce the monster to
My self, and then may be myself

In face of the monster.

1

There was this wound who loved its knife
And kept calling *Come back, come back,*
I am not deep enough,
And when it began to heal cried
Save me, I disappear.

2

A man looked for a long time
At something. Anything. He smelled it up close
And felt it all over and held it next to his ear
And shook it and then he licked it top to bottom.
He made a name for it. He put the name on a table,
And started to look at *it*. Then he smelled *it*
Up close, etc. By the time he put the name down again
He was kneeling. The thing he had made a name for
Was crushed under his knees but he didn't notice.
When it began to hurt his knees
He tried to stand up but couldn't.
He was speechless.

3

The numberless audience
Which never comes, which sits,
Out of whose hairshirts the sun rises,
Which longs for the moon to draw up
Its blood from their dreaming,
                                        whispers
As one body to itself

We win. We win.

HOMAGE TO MEDICINE BOW

He hid in the minds
of the people hunting him.

Imone mosey into your town, lonesomelike,
Looking no different from the image you have of me
In your flickering mind, disappointment
Riding low on my hips like sixguns,
Bitterness smoldering like a cigarette
Hanging from the slack side of my mouth,
Legend, that immutable dust, filming my boots
And saddle, my horse lathered
With ingenuity and repetition, over and
Over again
                    just like you've seen me do
Before, Imone ride into town, your town,
Destiny pulled low over my eyes like a Stetson,
Mercy alive in every fiber of my body
The way a Diamondback's rattlers are alive.

To that crackling song you'll see me dismount
Smoother'n a buzzard in updraft:
You will think the word *lingering* even after
I have sidled midway of Main Street,
The power alley of this egregious saga,
And watching my eyes flicker upward
To the lathed railings, the roof gardens
Of ambush, you will see in your frame of mind
The forked tongue of the soundtrack lick its air.
I will allow the future to hover
Like my hands over my hipguns, interminably,
Until everything's
                    ready
For whoever's
Scheduled this time, this first time
To stride suddenly from the shadows
Of the boardwalk, seeming to burst
Almost to light until at once
He arrests himself, catwalks, begins to move
Barely, a ballet of approach, until
The street admits him.
                    There he is,
A semblance.
                    Podnah the soundtrack says,

And in a tone of welcome again, *Podnah*, exactly
As you have heard, and the third voice, too,
Calls *Wait*, fatigue, lust, purity,
Cleanliness in the shape of a woman, calling *Wait*
And I will tell you,
                    that
Is what we would do, across the distance
We have created, we would bite neither the dust
Nor the bullet if we had our druthers,
We would wait
Simply, reality taut
Between us, in contention,
Doing what we do best.

But you won't bear expectation:
We draw, and one of us
Tomorrow, moseys into your town, lonesomelike.

THE WAY WEST

—The whirling noise
Of a multitude dwindles, all said,
To his breath that lies awake at night.

Whatever else misplaced desire
May do, it makes
An oblivion with too many lights,
Too many questions you have to ask, like
Whose shadow is this falling
Across the bed?   or *What time is it?*
To the clock with too many hands.
And that's just the beginning, one by one
The motes collect in the sunlight
Slanting, making angles with the blanket,
The walls, her settled ear. Dust grows
In the corners, while the shadows are content
To lean toward each other, clinking their glasses.

It's better to give up something for good
Than to spend years searching in a blind place
For what you've already got.

Let the lights go out, let them, one
By one, file out, leaving you
With the first circle, the signal fire.

A POLITICAL FABLE FOR PRACTICALLY
EVERYBODY

Once
Upon a time a little man who bustled mightily
And had a slippery tongue began to tell his friends
He had the whole world figured out, that it was
all
So simple. Everyone agreed that was wonderful,
The air thickened with congratulation,
But when I asked this centripetal person *What,*
Exactly, is so simple, a villainous question,
I earned exclusion from the simple
world.
Small world, I wonder,
A miniature prairie, rutted by infinitesimal wheels
Where the wind-up settlers had put their wagons in a circle
And fired briefly
Into a whirlwind of their own making?
May be.
His stirred-up speech, his location
Of the enemy outside that circle,
Lead me to say to him, waving
Across the appropriate divide,
Blow hard,
Old Buddy Shuffledust, wherever you go,
Wielding yourself, pure as a stone, and under my breath,
To whom all men who do not play by your rule
Are villainous.
I know
That bad cess
Is no civil farewell, but what else can you expect
From a villain?
Difficulty, for one thing,
and a certain
Hovering, a drawing toward, a passing into and through
When you least expect it. If he points at something,
Diverting your attention,
You have to remember his other three fingers
Curl back toward himself.

It was superior villainy of those Indians to sit
Their suspended ponies, out of range, watching

The settlers rifle their own circle, until the cloud
Of dust and motion rose skyward, insubstantial

As a vote.

THE ART OF POLITE CONVERSATION

I mumble something about the forms of nature
Being impermanent, the forms
Of cities being impermanent, the idea of form being
Impermanent.
                    I'm not she says.
                                    I can almost
Believe her in spite of the precedents, certain
Physical limitations
I don't need to catalogue:
                            she seems
So substantial, so
Impervious to the riddling years, so *cast*;
                                        as careless,
In fact, as the world she gallops through, her head
Averted from the wreckage, a brass smile
Turned to the audience, such thoroughgoing
Oblivion that if she brought down
Her gleeful quirt on her own back
She would wonder if it were raining.

Is it raining yet I ask under my breath
From under the table, having tried
Everything else I can think of.
                            No
She says, telling me her name.
                                    I'm ready
At last to let my mumbling fade,
Its echoes fade, leaving her a shape
The air might take, a rhythm teasing
The skin, breath,
                    this measure

Timed like any other, like goodbye.

STACKED UP OVER PARKERSBURG

Dearly departed, we are gathered together
Six planes higher than the clouds,
The tallest skyscraper in West Virginia

Suspended in a state of animation.

                       This is
Your captain speaking. No cause for alarm.
We are worthless except as we are worth something
To each other. I don't need to remind you
That what goes up etc. The planet will be there
Until further notice. Thank you for
Flying.

No matter how well those anonymous voices
Stroke the blank air, they comfort
No one, least of all me. Their promises
Can't compete with the variety of proof I watch
Outside this little window:
                      the flat top of the world
Filled with ice, the sincerity of its edges;
                          a circular
Sea breaking inward over its own shadow
Toward the point where it must absorb itself;
                           a monopoly
Of cotton banked by some invisible plow.
                     Even up here
There is too much history
                 nothing
Beside remains
               except the insistent image
Of repetition, repetition: the origin of slavery, of
Comfort. I almost want to ask the captain
To nestle into it forever, but his voice
Preempts me:
             Fasten
Your seatbelts, ladies and gentlemen, our troubles
Are over, we can speak again,
You may imagine the mouths of your lovers, the smell
Of bacon, your usual sleep. We have found
The quintessential rift: if you look down
You will see the shadow of our aircraft

Following us on the clouds; by the simplest
Of maneuvers we will now descend

Through it.

SHARP WORDS IN THE MEN'S ROOM

Does love end here? Or a man's work?
Here? Among this endless language?
                                        Clearly
From where I sit
The last word is a myth, and neither
Love nor work, that crossed
Conundrum, answers it.
                         As clearly,
Space divides according to a basic need
For—what? Privacy? To be privy
Only to one's necessities? To find
Among these partial stations time, anonymous
Concentration, for the simple move
That will make one rich, or to cry

Mommy in the dark as one possessed
Might seek to call forth from himself
His favorite mirror? It has resolved
Nothing; to judge from the writing on the walls
Neither has a siege of palpation and nibblement
Tidbitwise on the ticking. Nope.
                              Nevertheless, this is
A viable location, a verbal environment of some
Friendliness, a variable surround. Adjacent
To the tissue holder (empty in my stall)
The famous Big Bucks with Short Horns imperative
Reasserts itself; on the door so I may read it
From a commodious position is the modest maxim
Concerning the distance between literature
And the bowl (so to speak); elsewhere
Heartbreak and characterization occur,
Appointments are suggested, complete
With numbers for those inexperienced
In certain areas, and of course
There are the usual cave drawings depicting
Tribal customs and the dream life of the master race.

All the impressions are sizable, clearly
This is a place for people who care,
An imaginable community with a past, a forum—
                                              as I stood,
In fact, a shimmer of the air across the room

Appeared to coalesce into both wall and words,
A tablet, which I read aloud:

> When I began to love and fight
> I kept my language out of sight;
> Now that I own most of the world
> I prattle like a mindless girl.
> Does it always come to this, O Zeus,
> The upright staff, the torrid juice,
> Empire and *amor* politics
> Reduced to bathhouse limericks?
> It's too much for this verbose geezer
> Who signs *his* graffiti, Julius Caesar.

Ambitious, yes—more polished at least
Than the later scratchings I had previously
Encountered, but still
Local,
         tempered by the writer's immediate
Perplexity,
And neither weightier nor more historical than
Want some? Try Phyllis 771–1101.
                      I felt relieved. I
Zipped up, smoothed out, and shoved off,
                          elated
With the concert
Of human
Being
        and my part in it, all the way
In, I figure, doing what I can
To spread the word.

A CHANCE ENCOUNTER

Margin Morefingers, you old addict, bless your forearms.
There's no adequate cushion in this world, I know,
I know, but when a man takes it out on himself
He builds a hard place, a mold, too long a sacrifice,

And certain deaths become familiar, attractive,
Take on a sheen
Almost of art. Your eyes and mine begin
Watching your self, a screen
Where the parts of your life, shadowed,
Play themselves out.

              Where are we, unborn, in 1916, in Germany,

When seven men of various callings, prisoners of war,
Move about their cell—a room larger than this
With an escape tunnel in progress under the floor—
Move about separately, desultory, getting ready
For sleep, when they hear footsteps running across the stone
Courtyard, followed by shouts—*Halt, Schwein*—and shots:
Such a small margin, one bloody vowel, between
The voice of anger and its execution, and it brings
Those seven men at once, with one purpose, to themselves
As if they had no other, and to the window. As they watch
The guards drag off the body there is no stage, and yet
The camera withdraws slowly, withdrawing us, freezing them
Where they stand, suspended forever
In the frame of the window as if they would sing
Presently, or as if some college captains
Had gathered for the yearbook, all harmony
Before the dead:
           involuntary captains,
                    random alumni
Of some animate sublime, pure celluloid, pure mind.
                          Morefingers
Old Margin, they've helped make you the main attraction,
Network of a million private lives, the stage on which
Are played more daily dramas
Than any plausible universe could bear.

Just one more look,
At these grazed ghost towns, flickering. They
Were trips, too, manned flights exceeding
The budget, insidious trails to the future
Where the dust
Of the prairie may seem to outlast us all, filling
The silhouettes the actors left in the air,
Filling the air. We watch our own memory
Disperse. The sun sets among cacti, brutal, their spines
Glinting.
          If we draw back
From the set again, we can see a child
Of uncertain age sitting on the rug, stretching a skein
Of yarn between its hands, a kind of orbit,
While another of like uncertainty winds it into a ball.
It goes
On, it
Goes on,
          and here
Comes Morefingers, whose string never runs out,
A veritable spider, free sample, in spite of everything
Loping from one season to another, helpmeet
Of what unsuspecting clime, what virgin ink,

The great globe itself.

AN INTERLUDE AT THE GRAND HOTEL

This is no mailorder bride, nor a lyrical impulse
To be tricked out in beads and blossoms for a soupçon
Of matrimony *al fresco*. Nor a one-night stand.
Alone,
She looks across the lake toward something
Out of focus. Or at the air. If she removed
The broad-brimmed, filigreed hat, her brown hair
Would cascade all the way to her hips. Her lace cuffs
And the embroidered hem of her skirt
Edge the delicate bosses
Of her wrists and ankles, and her drawn waist
Moves slightly as she breathes. She is
Altogether composed.
                    The silhouette
Of privacy does not wish to entice,
As certain markings of butterflies have nothing
To do with the business of survival.
                            The woman
Looking across the still lake had a mind,
Too, for the attended life that's one long weave
Of unrecognized expectation.
                        The intricate
Crazings on this hotel porcelain
Weren't decorative, but a map of sensibility;
And these columns:
When she came here in the old days
She saw, without trying, the web of hairthin lines
In the marble, and called *that* marble. An eye for
The tenuous, the fine pattern of fragility
Along whose lines everything breaks, becoming
Visibly the pieces of itself it always was:
A crystalline vision,
                    the source of style.
                                I imagine
Her turning
Her head from the flat lake water and beginning to look
Down the long line of shore. The sunlight catches
A few wisps of hair, bronzing them, but
Her one visible eye remains in shadow.
                            She has
Breakfast in bed, the complacency of high ceilings;
A lover
Or not doesn't matter, the touch of flesh and sheet

Is sexual, cellular with longing.
The pores
Invite.
The breeze through the pines contends.
Her window
Has eighteen panes,
nor is the surface of the lake
glass.
The world promises nothing, because it is.

FINDING ONE OF THE GHOSTS

Love hid everywhere, including
The sour corners of his own memory;
He called to it, his voice reedy with longing,
But when he tried to confront it directly
He found nothing but salt talking.

Would I lure a rabbit with pork? he wondered.
Much less, then, love with promises.
He had given her more than he could promise
As it was, and what had it gotten him?

One mute servitude after another, bowing
Toward each vacuum she set before him
Until he hunched under the bottom shelf
Of the deepest closet, believing
Any brief crack in the door was morning.

It looked

Hopeless. *I might as well imagine*
The motion of a wing without a wing,
Or try to float a stone he said

And opened the door, wide, the simplest gesture.

After all
These years he had arrived at her level, and could look
Her in the eye.

It has taken me a while

To raise myself again through that surprise
But I am standing up now;
My eyes have adjusted to the light: I begin
To see a fading version of myself,
A suitcase in each hand, shuffling
Out the door, Old Baggy Pants, not quite
Chaplin, not quite my father. I wave
But he doesn't turn around,
Just keeps leaving. One day he'll be gone.

COMMON GROUND

It was a cool season, full of reserve
When the animals drew back
Into their memories, as if
They were hoarding something, saving it up
For the right time. There are no calendars
For such withdrawal, but perhaps
One of them saw its shadow
And ducked back down its hole, leaving the air
Shapeless with absence.
                 If you believe
Today is always an exception
                     you will never be a hero.

In an episode of The Wild Wild Old Days with Clever Gadgets
The heroine warns the hero, urgently, limpidly,
Not to go back in time with the villain whose mind
Controls matter, because he might never come back to the
                     present,
And the hero says, urgently, distantly, *If there is a 4th*
Dimension—and I believe there is—then I must
Find out if it is a threat
To the security of my country.

Everybody had trouble sleeping, the children
Were feverish for no apparent reason, birthday parties
Were canceled, pets of all kinds
Were still and silent,
                  there was a cortege of weather.

On another channel the captain of the spaceship
Told an alien life form who spoke his language
But whom he couldn't see (pure energy or something)
There's not room enough in this galaxy for both of us.

Dis make de udder Crawfishes mighty mad,
en dey sorter swarmed togedder en draw'd up
a kinder peramble wid some wharfo'es in it,
en read her out in de 'sembly. But, bless grashus!
sech a racket was a gwine on dat nobody ain't hear it,
'ceppin maybe de Mud Turkle en de Spring Lizzud,
en dere enfloons wuz pow'ful lackin'.
                     So dar dey wuz,
de Crawfishes, en dey didn't know w'at minnit

wuz gwinter be de nex'; en dey kep' on gittin madder
en madder en skeerder en skeerder, twel bimeby
dey gun de wink ter de Mud Turkle en de Spring Lizzud,
en den dey bo'd little holes in de groun' en went down

outer sight.

                If the earth were someday
Filled with the pressure of such shrewd joy,
                                what
Fountains there would be, what
Flowing. The ladies would sashay and the children
Gambol, old words bloom. Even now it wells up:

This child of mine lies on his side on the floor,
One leg drawn up under the other,
His head resting on a forearm,
Listening.